This Mushroom Hunting LogBook Belongs To:

"To walk into nature is to witness a thousand miracles."

Mary Davis

My Mushroom Hunting Adventures

Date:_____

Location:_____
_____

Facing Direction:_____

Temperature and Weather Conditions:

_____
_____

Species of Trees in the Area:

_____
_____

Burn Zone:
Yes_____
No_____

Downed or Dead Trees:
Yes_____
No_____

Soil Conditions:_____

MY Mushroom Haul

Species	Size	Quantity

Sketches & Photos of What I Found

Musings & Memories

My Mushroom Hunting Adventures

Date:_____

Location:_____

_____

Facing Direction:_____

Temperature and Weather Conditions:

_____

_____

Species of Trees in the Area:

_____

_____

Burn Zone:
Yes_____
No_____

Downed or Dead Trees:
Yes_____
No_____

Soil Conditions:_____

My Mushroom Haul

Species	Size	Quantity

Sketches & Photos of What I Found

Musings & Memories

My Mushroom Hunting Adventures

Date:_____

Location:_____
_____

Facing Direction:_____

Temperature and Weather Conditions:

_____

_____

Species of Trees in the Area:

_____

_____

Burn Zone:
Yes_____
No_____

Downed or Dead Trees:
Yes_____
No_____

Soil Conditions:_____

MY Mushroom Haul

Species	Size	Quantity

Sketches & Photos of What I Found

Musings & Memories

My Mushroom Hunting Adventures

Date:_____

Location:_____

_____

Facing Direction:_____

Temperature and Weather Conditions:

_____

_____

Species of Trees in the Area:

_____

_____

Burn Zone:

Yes_____

No_____

Downed or Dead Trees:

Yes_____

No_____

Soil Conditions:_____

My Mushroom Haul

Species	Size	Quantity

Sketches & Photos of What I Found

Musings & Memories

My Mushroom Hunting Adventures

Date:_____

Location:_____

_____

Facing Direction:_____

Temperature and Weather Conditions:

_____

_____

Species of Trees in the Area:

_____

_____

Burn Zone:
Yes_____
No_____

Downed or Dead Trees:
Yes_____
No_____

Soil Conditions:_____

MY Mushroom Haul

Species	Size	Quantity

Sketches & Photos of What I Found

Musings & Memories

My Mushroom Hunting Adventures

Date:_____

Location:_____

_____

Facing Direction:_____

Temperature and Weather Conditions:

_____

_____

Species of Trees in the Area:

_____

_____

Burn Zone:
Yes_____
No_____

Downed or Dead Trees:
Yes_____
No_____

Soil Conditions:_____

MY Mushroom Haul

Species	Size	Quantity

Sketches & Photos of What I Found

Musings & Memories

My Mushroom Hunting Adventures

Date:_____

Location:_____

_____

Facing Direction:_____

Temperature and Weather Conditions:

_____

_____

Species of Trees in the Area:

_____

_____

Burn Zone:

Yes_____

No_____

Downed or Dead Trees:

Yes_____

No_____

Soil Conditions:_____

MY Mushroom Haul

Species	Size	Quantity

Sketches & Photos of What I Found

Musings & Memories

My Mushroom Hunting Adventures

Date:_____

Location:_____
_____

Facing Direction:_____

Temperature and Weather Conditions:

_____

_____

Species of Trees in the Area:

_____

_____

Burn Zone:
Yes_____
No_____

Downed or Dead Trees:
Yes_____
No_____

Soil Conditions:_____

MY Mushroom Haul

Species	Size	Quantity

Sketches & Photos of What I Found

Musings & Memories

My Mushroom Hunting Adventures

Date:_____

Location:_____
_____

Facing Direction:_____

Temperature and Weather Conditions:

_____

_____

Species of Trees in the Area:

_____

_____

Burn Zone:
Yes_____
No_____

Downed or Dead Trees:
Yes_____
No_____

Soil Conditions:_____

My Mushroom Haul

Species	Size	Quantity

Sketches & Photos of What I Found

Musings & Memories

My Mushroom Hunting Adventures

Date:_____

Location:_____

_____

Facing Direction:_____

Temperature and Weather Conditions:

_____

_____

Species of Trees in the Area:

_____

_____

Burn Zone:
Yes_____
No_____

Downed or Dead Trees:
Yes_____
No_____

Soil Conditions:_____

MY Mushroom Haul

Species	Size	Quantity

Sketches & Photos of What I Found

Musings & Memories

My Mushroom Hunting Adventures

Date:_____

Location:_____

_____

Facing Direction:_____

Temperature and Weather Conditions:

_____

_____

Species of Trees in the Area:

_____

_____

Burn Zone:
Yes_____
No_____

Downed or Dead Trees:
Yes_____
No_____

Soil Conditions:_____

My Mushroom Haul

Species	Size	Quantity

Sketches & Photos of What I Found

Musings & Memories

My Mushroom Hunting Adventures

Date:_____

Location:_____
_____

Facing Direction:_____

Temperature and Weather Conditions:
_____
_____

Species of Trees in the Area:
_____
_____

Burn Zone:
Yes_____
No_____

Downed or Dead Trees:
Yes_____
No_____

Soil Conditions:_____

MY Mushroom Haul

Species	Size	Quantity

Sketches & Photos of What I Found

Musings & Memories

My Mushroom Hunting Adventures

Date:_____

Location:_____

_____

Facing Direction:_____

Temperature and Weather Conditions:

_____

_____

Species of Trees in the Area:

_____

_____

Burn Zone:

Yes_____

No_____

Downed or Dead Trees:

Yes_____

No_____

Soil Conditions:_____

My Mushroom Haul

Species	Size	Quantity

Sketches & Photos of What I Found

Musings & Memories

My Mushroom Hunting Adventures

Date:_____

Location:_____

_____

Facing Direction:_____

Temperature and Weather Conditions:

_____

_____

Species of Trees in the Area:

_____

_____

Burn Zone:

Yes_____

No_____

Downed or Dead Trees:

Yes_____

No_____

Soil Conditions:_____

My Mushroom Haul

Species	Size	Quantity

Sketches & Photos of What I Found

Musings & Memories

MY Mushroom Hunting Adventures

Date:_____

Location:_____

_____

Facing Direction:_____

Temperature and Weather Conditions:

_____

_____

Species of Trees in the Area:

_____

_____

Burn Zone:
Yes_____
No_____

Downed or Dead Trees:
Yes_____
No_____

Soil Conditions:_____

MY Mushroom Haul

Species	Size	Quantity

Sketches & Photos of What I Found

Musings & Memories

My Mushroom Hunting Adventures

Date:_____

Location:_____
_____

Facing Direction:_____

Temperature and Weather Conditions:
_____
_____

Species of Trees in the Area:
_____
_____

Burn Zone:
Yes_____
No_____

Downed or Dead Trees:
Yes_____
No_____

Soil Conditions:_____

My Mushroom Haul

Species	Size	Quantity

Sketches & Photos of What I Found

Musings & Memories

My Mushroom Hunting Adventures

Date:_____

Location:_____

_____

Facing Direction:_____

Temperature and Weather Conditions:

_____

_____

Species of Trees in the Area:

_____

_____

Burn Zone:
Yes_____
No_____

Downed or Dead Trees:
Yes_____
No_____

Soil Conditions:_____

MY Mushroom Haul

Species	Size	Quantity

Sketches & Photos of What I Found

Musings & Memories

My Mushroom Hunting Adventures

Date:_____

Location:_____
_____

Facing Direction:_____

Temperature and Weather Conditions:
_____
_____

Species of Trees in the Area:
_____
_____

Burn Zone:
Yes_____
No_____

Downed or Dead Trees:
Yes_____
No_____

Soil Conditions:_____

MY Mushroom Haul

Species	Size	Quantity

Sketches & Photos of What I Found

Musings & Memories

My Mushroom Hunting Adventures

Date:_____

Location:_____

_____

Facing Direction:_____

Temperature and Weather Conditions:

_____

_____

Species of Trees in the Area:

_____

_____

Burn Zone:

Yes_____

No_____

Downed or Dead Trees:

Yes_____

No_____

Soil Conditions:_____

MY Mushroom Haul

Species	Size	Quantity

Sketches & Photos of What I Found

Musings & Memories

My Mushroom Hunting Adventures

Date:_____

Location:_____

_____

Facing Direction:_____

Temperature and Weather Conditions:

_____

_____

Species of Trees in the Area:

_____

_____

Burn Zone:

Yes_____

No_____

Downed or Dead Trees:

Yes_____

No_____

Soil Conditions:_____

My Mushroom Haul

Species	Size	Quantity

Sketches & Photos of What I Found

Musings & Memories

My Mushroom Hunting Adventures

Date:_____

Location:_____

_____

Facing Direction:_____

Temperature and Weather Conditions:

_____

_____

Species of Trees in the Area:

_____

_____

Burn Zone:
Yes_____
No_____

Downed or Dead Trees:
Yes_____
No_____

Soil Conditions:_____

MY Mushroom Haul

Species	Size	Quantity

Sketches & Photos of What I Found

Musings & Memories

My Mushroom Hunting Adventures

Date:_____

Location:_____

_____

Facing Direction:_____

Temperature and Weather Conditions:

_____

_____

Species of Trees in the Area:

_____

_____

Burn Zone:
Yes_____
No_____

Downed or Dead Trees:
Yes_____
No_____

Soil Conditions:_____

MY Mushroom Haul

Species	Size	Quantity

Sketches & Photos of What I Found

Musings & Memories

My Mushroom Hunting Adventures

Date:_____

Location:_____

_____

Facing Direction:_____

Temperature and Weather Conditions:

_____

_____

Species of Trees in the Area:

_____

_____

Burn Zone:
Yes_____
No_____

Downed or Dead Trees:
Yes_____
No_____

Soil Conditions:_____

My Mushroom Haul

Species	Size	Quantity

Sketches & Photos of What I Found

Musings & Memories

My Mushroom Hunting Adventures

Date:_____

Location:_____

_____

Facing Direction:_____

Temperature and Weather Conditions:

_____

_____

Species of Trees in the Area:

_____

_____

Burn Zone:

Yes_____

No_____

Downed or Dead Trees:

Yes_____

No_____

Soil Conditions:_____

My Mushroom Haul

Species	Size	Quantity

Sketches & Photos of What I Found

Musings & Memories

My Mushroom Hunting Adventures

Date:_____

Location:_____

_____

Facing Direction:_____

Temperature and Weather Conditions:

_____

_____

Species of Trees in the Area:

_____

_____

Burn Zone:
Yes_____
No_____

Downed or Dead Trees:
Yes_____
No_____

Soil Conditions:_____

My Mushroom Haul

Species	Size	Quantity

Sketches & Photos of What I Found

Musings & Memories

My Mushroom Hunting Adventures

Date:_____

Location:_____

_____

Facing Direction:_____

Temperature and Weather Conditions:

_____

_____

Species of Trees in the Area:

_____

_____

Burn Zone:
Yes_____
No_____

Downed or Dead Trees:
Yes_____
No_____

Soil Conditions:_____

My Mushroom Haul

Species	Size	Quantity

Sketches & Photos of What I Found

Musings & Memories

My Mushroom Hunting Adventures

Date:_____

Location:_____

_____

Facing Direction:_____

Temperature and Weather Conditions:

_____

_____

Species of Trees in the Area:

_____

_____

Burn Zone:
Yes_____
No_____

Downed or Dead Trees:
Yes_____
No_____

Soil Conditions:_____

My Mushroom Haul

Species	Size	Quantity

Sketches & Photos of What I Found

Musings & Memories

MY Mushroom Hunting Adventures

Date:_____

Location:_____

_____

Facing Direction:_____

Temperature and Weather Conditions:

_____

_____

Species of Trees in the Area:

_____

_____

Burn Zone:

Yes_____

No_____

Downed or Dead Trees:

Yes_____

No_____

Soil Conditions:_____

My Mushroom Haul

Species	Size	Quantity

Sketches & Photos of What I Found

Musings & Memories

My Mushroom Hunting Adventures

Date:_____

Location:_____

_____

Facing Direction:_____

Temperature and Weather Conditions:

_____

_____

Species of Trees in the Area:

_____

_____

Burn Zone:

Yes_____

No_____

Downed or Dead Trees:

Yes_____

No_____

Soil Conditions:_____

My Mushroom Haul

Species	Size	Quantity

Sketches & Photos of What I Found

Musings & Memories

My Mushroom Hunting Adventures

Date:_____

Location:_____

_____

Facing Direction:_____

Temperature and Weather Conditions:

_____

_____

Species of Trees in the Area:

_____

_____

Burn Zone:

Yes_____

No_____

Downed or Dead Trees:

Yes_____

No_____

Soil Conditions:_____

MY Mushroom Haul

Species	Size	Quantity

Sketches & Photos of What I Found

Musings & Memories

My Mushroom Hunting Adventures

Date:_____

Location:_____

_____

Facing Direction:_____

Temperature and Weather Conditions:

_____

_____

Species of Trees in the Area:

_____

_____

Burn Zone:
Yes_____
No_____

Downed or Dead Trees:
Yes_____
No_____

Soil Conditions:_____

MY Mushroom Haul

Species	Size	Quantity

Sketches & Photos of What I Found

Musings & Memories

My Mushroom Hunting Adventures

Date:_____

Location:_____

_____

Facing Direction:_____

Temperature and Weather Conditions:

_____

_____

Species of Trees in the Area:

_____

_____

Burn Zone:

Yes_____

No_____

Downed or Dead Trees:

Yes_____

No_____

Soil Conditions:_____

MY Mushroom Haul

Species	Size	Quantity

Sketches & Photos of What I Found

Musings & Memories

My Mushroom Hunting Adventures

Date:_____

Location:_____

_____

Facing Direction:_____

Temperature and Weather Conditions:

_____

_____

Species of Trees in the Area:

_____

_____

Burn Zone:

Yes_____

No_____

Downed or Dead Trees:

Yes_____

No_____

Soil Conditions:_____

My Mushroom Haul

Species	Size	Quantity

Sketches & Photos of What I Found

Musings & Memories

Time to head back to Amazon to order another book. If you enjoyed this mushroom hunting logbook, we hope you will share your opinion by leaving a review on Amazon.
Thank you,
Wandering Trails

Made in United States
North Haven, CT
17 July 2022